Make Money on Etsy

Introduction

Etsy is an online marketplace founded in 2005 by Robert Kalin, Chris Maguire, and Haim Schoppik. The company was initially focused on handmade and vintage goods and was inspired by the founder's desire to create a platform that would support small-scale, independent artisans and creators.

The company launched in 2005 and quickly gained popularity, with more than 45,000 registered sellers by the end of the year. In 2006, Etsy received its first round of funding, and in 2007, the company launched its first international site, targeting the UK market.

In the years that followed, Etsy continued to grow and expand, introducing new features and categories to the platform. Today, the company has over 2.7 million active sellers and 60 million active buyers and operates in over 200 countries.

Etsy has also made a commitment to sustainability, with a focus on promoting responsible and ethical business practices. The company has implemented a range of initiatives to support sustainability, including the development of an environmental sustainability program and the launch of a carbon offset program.

Etsy also operates in a number of countries around the world, including the United Kingdom, Germany, and Canada. Here is a brief overview of Etsy in each of these countries:

United Kingdom: Etsy has a strong presence in the UK, with a dedicated UK website and a large community of sellers and buyers. The company has offices in London and has a range of initiatives to support UK sellers, including a UK seller handbook and a range of tools and resources to help sellers grow their businesses.

Germany: Etsy also has a strong presence in Germany, with a dedicated German website and a large community of sellers and buyers. The company has an office in Berlin and has a range of initiatives to support German sellers, including a German seller handbook and a range of tools and resources to help sellers grow their businesses.

Canada: Etsy has a significant presence in Canada, with a dedicated Canadian website and a large community of sellers and buyers. The company has an office in Toronto and has a range of initiatives to support Canadian sellers, including a Canadian seller handbook and a range of tools and resources to help sellers grow their businesses.

A few examples of services that Etsy offers:

1. Listing and selling products: Etsy provides a platform for sellers to list and sell their handmade, vintage, and creative goods. Sellers can create product listings, manage inventory, and process orders through Etsy's platform.

2. Marketing and advertising: Etsy offers a range of tools and resources to help sellers promote their products and reach a wider audience. This includes SEO tools, promoted listings, and targeted advertising.

3. Payment processing: Etsy provides a secure payment processing system for sellers, allowing them to accept payments from buyers through the platform.

4. Customer support: Etsy offers customer support to sellers and buyers through its help center, which includes a range of resources and tools to help users troubleshoot problems and resolve issues.

5. Shipping and fulfillment: Etsy provides shipping and fulfillment services to sellers through its Etsy Shipping Labels and Etsy Fulfillment services. These services allow sellers to easily print shipping labels and manage orders through the platform.

Here are a few testimonials from successful Etsy sellers:

1. "I started selling on Etsy as a hobby, and it quickly turned into a full-time business. I love the creative freedom that Etsy provides, and I've been able to build a loyal customer

base through the platform. I'm so grateful for the opportunity that Etsy has given me to turn my passion into a successful business."
2. "I never thought I'd be able to turn my hobby into a full-time career, but with the help of Etsy, I've been able to do just that. I've been able to connect with a global audience and build a strong customer base, and I'm so grateful for the opportunity that Etsy has given me to grow my business."
3. "Etsy has been a game-changer for my business. I've been able to reach a much larger audience than I ever could have on my own, and the support and resources provided by the platform have been invaluable. I'm so grateful to be able to do what I love every day, and I wouldn't have been able to do it without Etsy."

These testimonials demonstrate that Etsy can be a valuable platform for building a successful business and turning a passion into a career.
Good luck!

Chapter 1: Setting up your shop

Welcome to the world of Etsy! If you are reading this, you are probably interested in starting an Etsy shop and making some extra money. Etsy is a great platform for creative entrepreneurs to sell their handmade or vintage items, and it has a huge customer base. In this book, we will go over the steps you need to take to get your shop up and running, as well as some tips and strategies for success. Let's get started!
Etsy is a marketplace for handmade, vintage, and unique goods. Some examples of items that can be sold on Etsy include

1. Handmade items, such as jewelry, clothing, home decor, and accessories
2. Vintage items, such as clothing, furniture, and collectibles
3. Art prints and original artwork
4. Craft supplies, such as beads, fabric, and patterns
5. Handmade soaps and beauty products

6. Wedding and party supplies, such as invitations, favors, and decorations
7. Baby items, such as clothing, toys, and accessories
8. Handmade furniture
9. Handmade toys
10. Health and wellness products
11. Outdoor gear and equipment
12. Books and journals
13. Handmade candles
14. Handmade paper products
15. Handmade pet toys

Here is a list of some of the main product categories on Etsy:

1. Clothing and accessories: This category includes a range of handmade and vintage clothing, such as dresses, tops, and bottoms, as well as accessories, such as bags, scarves, and hats.
2. Home and living: This category includes a range of handmade and vintage home decor items, such as furniture, bedding, and rugs, as well as products for the kitchen, such as dishes and cooking utensils.
3. Jewelry: This category includes a range of handmade and vintage jewelry, such as rings, earrings, and necklaces.
4. Art and collectibles: This category includes a range of handmade and vintage art and collectibles, such as paintings, prints, and sculptures.
5. Craft supplies: This category includes a range of supplies for crafting, such as fabric, yarn, and beads.
6. Wedding: This category includes a range of products for weddings, such as invitations, favors, and decor.
7. Toys and games: This category includes a range of handmade and vintage toys and games, such as dolls, puzzles, and board games.
8. Electronics and accessories: This category includes a range of handmade and vintage electronics and accessories, such as phone cases and chargers.

There are several benefits to selling on Etsy, including:

1. Access to a global audience: Etsy is a popular online
    marketplace that attracts buyers from around the world.
    By selling on Etsy, you can reach a global audience and
    potentially increase your sales.
2. Low upfront costs: It's relatively inexpensive to start
    selling on Etsy, as there are no monthly fees or
    membership costs. You only pay a small listing fee and a
    transaction fee when you make a sale.
3. Built-in customer support: Etsy offers a range of tools and
    resources to help sellers manage their businesses,
    including customer support, marketing, and order
    management tools.
4. Strong seller community: Etsy has a strong seller
    community that offers support and resources to help
    sellers grow their businesses.
5. Established reputation: Etsy has a well-established
    reputation as a trusted online marketplace, which can help
    increase customer confidence in your products.

There are several reasons why some sellers may prefer to sell on
Etsy instead of eBay:

1. Targeted audience: Etsy is a marketplace specifically
    geared towards handmade, vintage, and creative goods, so
    sellers on the platform may have an easier time reaching a
    targeted audience of buyers interested in these types of
    products.
2. Lower fees: Etsy charges lower fees than eBay, making it
    potentially more profitable for sellers.
3. Better seller support: Etsy offers a range of tools and
    resources to help sellers manage their businesses,
    including customer support, marketing, and order
    management tools. Some sellers may find this support to
    be more comprehensive than what is offered by eBay.

4. Strong seller community: Etsy has a strong seller community that offers support and resources to help sellers grow their businesses.
5. Established reputation: Etsy has a well-established reputation as a trusted online marketplace, which can help increase customer confidence in your products.

Ultimately, the decision to sell on Etsy or eBay will depend on your specific business needs and goals. By selling on Etsy, you can take advantage of these benefits and potentially grow your business. eBay and Amazon are all online marketplaces that allow sellers to sell their products to a global audience. However, there are some key differences between the three platforms:

1. Product categories: Etsy primarily focuses on handmade, vintage, and unique goods, while eBay and Amazon have a wider range of categories, including new and used items.
2. Fees: Etsy charges a listing fee and a transaction fee for each sale, while eBay and Amazon have different fee structures based on the category of the product and the seller's selling plan.
3. Customer base: Etsy has a dedicated customer base of shoppers looking for handmade and unique products, while eBay and Amazon have a wider range of customers.
4. Selling process: Etsy has a more streamlined selling process, with tools and resources specifically designed for handmade and unique goods. eBay and Amazon have more complex selling processes, with a wider range of product categories and more stringent requirements for sellers.

By understanding the differences between these platforms, you can choose the one that best fits your product offerings and business goals.
As of 2021, it costs $0.20 to list an item for sale on Etsy. This listing fee is charged every time you list an item, and it is valid for four months or until the item is sold, whichever comes first.
In addition to the listing fee, Etsy also charges a transaction fee for each sale made through the platform. This fee is calculated as a

percentage of the sale price, and it is currently 5% for most products.

It's important to note that these fees are in addition to any payment processing fees that may be charged by Etsy's payment partners. These fees may vary depending on the payment method used by the buyer and the location of the seller.

The fees to list and sell items on Etsy are generally considered relatively low compared to other online marketplaces. This can make it a cost-effective platform for sellers looking to reach a large and diverse customer base.

The first step to making money on Etsy is setting up your shop. This involves creating a seller account, choosing a shop name and branding, and setting up your payment and shipping options.

To create a seller account, go to the Etsy homepage and click on the "Sell on Etsy" button. Follow the prompts to create your account and set up your shop.

Next, choose a shop name and branding that reflects the products you will be selling. This can be your own name or a catchy name related to your products.

Finally, set up your payment and shipping options. Etsy allows you to accept payments through PayPal and credit cards, and you can choose your preferred shipping carriers and rates.

Whether or not you need to hire a lawyer and accountant for your Etsy store will depend on the specific needs and goals of your business. Here are a few factors to consider:

1. Legal considerations: If you are selling physical products on Etsy, you may want to consider hiring a lawyer to help with contract drafting and review, intellectual property issues, and other legal matters.
2. Tax considerations: If you are making a significant amount of money from your Etsy store, you may consider hiring an accountant to help you with tax planning and compliance. An accountant can also help you with bookkeeping and financial reporting.
3. Business structure: If you are planning to expand your Etsy store into a larger business, you may want to consider hiring a lawyer to help you choose the right business structure (e.g., sole proprietorship, partnership, corporation) and handle any legal matters related to setting up your business.

Ultimately, the decision to hire a lawyer and accountant for your Etsy store will depend on your specific needs and goals. It's a good idea to carefully assess your business and consult with professionals to ensure you have the support and guidance you need to succeed.

Etsy Star Sellers are Etsy sellers who have consistently received high ratings and reviews from their customers. To become an Etsy Star Seller, a seller must meet the following criteria:

1. Have at least 100 sales on Etsy within the last 12 months.
2. Have a rating of 4.5 or higher.
3. Have a completion rate of 90% or higher.

Etsy Star Sellers receive a badge on their shop page and in their search results to help them stand out to buyers. This can potentially increase their visibility and credibility on the platform. Etsy Star Sellers may also have access to additional resources and support from Etsy to help them grow their businesses.

Being an Etsy Star Seller can provide a number of benefits, including increased visibility and credibility, access to additional resources and support, and the potential to attract more customers and grow your business.

Tips for opening a successful online store on Etsy:

1. Choose a niche: Choose a niche or category for your store that you are passionate about and have knowledge or expertise in. This will help you create unique and high-quality products that stand out in the market.
2. Create a brand: Develop a brand identity for your store, including a logo, color scheme, and style. This will help you create a cohesive look for your products and establish a professional image.
3. Research your competition: Research other stores in your niche to see what products and prices they offer. This will

help you understand the market and create a competitive pricing strategy.

4. Source materials carefully: Choose high-quality materials and supplies that fit your brand's aesthetic and price point.

5. Set up your store: Set up your store on Etsy by creating a seller account and listing your products. Include detailed descriptions, high-quality photos, and accurate pricing for your products.

6. Promote your store: Promote your store through social media, email marketing, and other channels to reach a wider audience. Consider offering discounts or promotions to encourage sales.

7. Engage with your customers: Make sure to respond to customer inquiries and reviews in a timely and professional manner. Building a positive reputation with your customers can help drive sales and increase customer loyalty.

Tips for finding a good, catchy, and easy-to-remember store name:

1. Keep it simple: Choose a store name that is easy to spell and pronounce. A simple name is more likely to be remembered and shared by customers.

2. Make it memorable: Choose a store name that is unique and memorable. A memorable name can help you stand out in the market and make it easier for customers to find your store.

3. Avoid using numbers or special characters: Avoid using numbers or special characters in your store name, as they can be difficult to remember and may not be searchable.

4. Use keywords: Consider including keywords related to your products or niche in your store name to help customers find your store through search engines.

5. Consider your brand: Choose a store name that reflects your brand and the products you offer. This can help

customers understand what they can expect from your store.

Here are a few catchy store names that could be used on Etsy:

1. "Hip and Handmade"
2. "Vintage Visions"
3. "Crafty Creations"
4. "Eco-Chic Boutique"
5. "Artfully Unique"
6. "The Boho Market"
7. "The Rustic Way"
8. "Upcycled Treasures"
9. "The Creative Corner"
10. "Sustainable Style"

These store names are meant to be catchy and memorable while also giving a sense of the types of products that might be sold in the store.

There are several affordable or free tax software options available for Etsy sellers:

1. TaxJar: This tax software offers a range of plans for Etsy sellers, including a free plan that includes sales tax calculation, tax reporting, and basic support.
2. Taxify: This tax software offers a range of plans for Etsy sellers, including a free plan that includes sales tax calculation and basic support.
3. TaxAct: This tax software offers a range of plans for Etsy sellers, including a free plan that includes sales tax calculation and basic support.
4. H&R Block: This tax software offers a range of plans for Etsy sellers, including a free plan that includes sales tax calculation and basic support.
5. QuickBooks Self-Employed: This tax software offers a range of plans for Etsy sellers, including a free plan that includes sales tax calculation, tax reporting, and basic support.

By using one of these affordable or free tax software options, you can easily track and report your sales tax obligations as an Etsy seller. It's important to carefully research and compares the different options to determine the best fit for your business.

It is not required to have a business card or company logo to open a store on Etsy. However, having these items can help you establish a professional image for your business and make it easier for customers to remember and find your store.

A business card is a small card that includes your business name, contact information, and any other relevant details about your business. You can use business cards to share your store information with potential customers and network with other business owners.

A company logo is a graphical element that, together with its logotype or typeface, forms a trademark or commercial brand. Typically, a logo is a symbol or design that represents a company or product. Having a company logo can help customers easily identify your business and products and can also help you establish a professional image.

While it is not required to have a business card or company logo to open a store on Etsy, it is a good idea to consider these elements as you build and promote your business.

Chapter 2: Listing your products

To list items on Etsy, follow these steps:

1. Set up an Etsy account: Go to Etsy.com and click on the "Sell on Etsy" button to create an account. You will need to provide your email address, create a password, and agree to Etsy's terms of use.
2. Create your shop: Once you have an account, you can start setting up your shop. You will need to choose a shop name, create a banner and profile image, and set your location and currency.
3. Add listings: To add a listing to your shop, click on the "Listings" tab and then click on the "Add a listing" button. You will need to enter the following information for each listing:

- Title: Choose a title that accurately describes your item and includes relevant keywords.
- Description: Write a detailed description of your item, including its materials, dimensions, and unique features.
- Photos: Add high-quality photos of your item from multiple angles.
- Category: Choose the most relevant category for your item.
- Tags: Add tags to your listing to make it easier for customers to find your item.
- Pricing: Enter the price for your item and choose whether to include shipping costs in the price or charge for shipping separately.

4. Publish your listing: Once you have completed all the necessary information, click on the "Publish" button to make your listing live on Etsy.

5. Set up payment and shipping options: To accept payment from customers and ship your items, you will need to set up payment and shipping options in your shop. You can choose to accept credit card payments through Etsy, or you can link your shop to a PayPal account. You will also need to choose your preferred shipping carriers and set your shipping rates.

The appropriate markup for a product in an online store depends on various factors, including the cost of the product, the market demand for the product, and the competition in the market. Generally, a markup of 50-100% is considered reasonable for most products. However, it's important to do your research and consider the specific market conditions for your products when determining your markup.

A few tips for determining a reasonable markup for your products:

1. Calculate your costs: Determine the cost of producing and sourcing your products, including materials, labor, and other expenses.
2. Consider your target market: Research the demand for your products and the competition in your market to determine the appropriate price point for your products.
3. Determine your profit margin: Calculate your desired profit margin and use it to determine the appropriate markup for your products. For example, if you want to achieve a profit margin of 25%, you must mark up your products by approximately 50%.

By considering these factors, you can determine a reasonable markup for your products that will help you achieve your desired profit margin while still offering a competitive price to your customers.

Example of a customer policy for an online store on Etsy:

Welcome to our store! We are dedicated to providing the best possible shopping experience for our customers. If you have any questions or concerns, please don't hesitate to contact us.
Order Processing:

- All orders are processed within 1-3 business days, unless otherwise noted in the item listing.
- Custom orders may take longer to process and ship, and the turnaround time will be specified in the item listing.

Shipping:

- We offer both domestic and international shipping.
- Shipping rates are calculated based on the weight and size of the package, as well as the destination.
- All orders are shipped via USPS or UPS, and tracking information will be provided once the order has shipped.
- Please allow for potential delays due to COVID-19 or other unforeseen circumstances.

Returns:

- If unsatisfied with your purchase, please contact us within seven days of receiving your order to request a return exchange.
- Returns must be in their original condition, with all tags and packaging intact.
- Custom orders are not eligible for returns or exchanges.
- The buyer is responsible for return shipping costs.

Cancellations:

- If you need to cancel your order, please contact us as soon as possible.
- If your order has already shipped, it cannot be canceled.

Custom Orders:

- We offer custom orders for select products.
- Custom orders require a 50% deposit, which is non-refundable.
- The turnaround time for custom orders will be specified in the listing.

Privacy:

- We value your privacy and will not share your personal information with third parties.
- Your information will only be used for the purpose of processing and shipping your order.

Thank you for shopping with us! We appreciate your business and look forward to serving you again in the future.

Chapter 3: Finding your niche

Having a niche is important for a number of reasons when it comes to becoming a successful Etsy seller. Here are a few reasons why:

1. Targeted marketing: By focusing on a specific niche, you can more effectively target your marketing efforts to reach the right customers. This can help you stand out in a crowded marketplace and attract buyers specifically interested in the types of products you offer.
2. Brand identity: Having a niche can help you establish a clear brand identity and position yourself as an expert in your field. This can help you build customer trust and loyalty.
3. Increased competition: Specializing in a specific niche can help you stand out in a crowded marketplace and differentiate yourself from competitors. By focusing on a specific area, you can potentially face less competition and increase your chances of success.
4. Product development: Focusing on a specific niche can help you identify opportunities for product development and innovation. This can help you stay ahead of trends and keep your products fresh and relevant to your target audience.

A niche can help you effectively market and grow your business on Etsy. It's important to carefully research and consider the specific market conditions and demand for your products before choosing a niche.

1. Determine your interests and passions: The first step in finding your niche on Etsy is to think about what you enjoy creating or working with. What are your hobbies or interests? What are you knowledgeable about or passionate about? Consider the things that make you happy and excited to create.
2. Research market trends and customer demand: Once you have identified your interests, it's important to research market trends and customer demand to ensure a market for your products. Look at popular categories on Etsy, as well as Google trends, to see what types of products are currently in demand.
3. Consider your unique skills and abilities: What sets you apart from other sellers on Etsy? Do you have a unique skill or talent that you can showcase in your products? This could be a particular craft technique, a specialized knowledge of a certain material, or a particular design style.
4. Look for gaps in the market: Is there a particular product or category that is underrepresented on Etsy? If so, this could be a great opportunity for you to fill that gap and stand out from the competition.
5. Test out different ideas: Don't be afraid to experiment with different product ideas to see what works best for your business. You can use social media or a small group of friends or family to gauge interest and get feedback on your products.
6. Narrow down your focus: Once you have a list of potential product ideas, try narrowing your focus to a specific niche. It can be helpful to choose a niche that is specific enough to stand out but broad enough to offer a range of products.
7. Consider your target audience: Who is your ideal customer? What are their interests and needs? Consider your target audience when choosing your niche, as this will help you create products that appeal to them.
8. Choose a niche that aligns with your values: It's important to choose a niche that aligns with your personal values and beliefs. This will make it easier to stay motivated and committed to your business and will also help you connect with customers who share your values.

9. Don't be afraid to pivot: It's okay if your initial niche doesn't work out or if you change your mind. Your business will evolve and change over time, and that's okay. Be open to pivoting and adapting as needed.
10. Get feedback from others: Finally, don't be afraid to ask for feedback from others, including other Etsy sellers or potential customers. Their insights can be valuable in helping you refine your niche and create products that will sell well on Etsy.

50 potential niches to sell products on Etsy:

1. Handmade jewelry
2. Home decor
3. Baby products
4. Wedding and party supplies
5. Art prints and original artwork
6. Handmade soap and beauty products
7. Clothing and accessories
8. Bags and purses
9. Vintage items
10. Handmade furniture
11. Kitchen and dining products
12. Pet products
13. Office supplies and stationery
14. Handmade toys
15. Health and wellness products
16. Outdoor gear and equipment
17. Books and journals
18. Handmade candles
19. Handmade paper products
20. Handmade pet toys
21. Handmade gifts and gift baskets
22. Handmade skincare products
23. Handmade home fragrances

24. Handmade bath and body products
25. Handmade pottery and ceramics
26. Handmade baskets
27. Handmade musical instruments
28. Handmade plant pots and planters
29. Handmade phone cases
30. Handmade beauty tools
31. Handmade pet beds
32. Handmade quilts and blankets
33. Handmade wedding invitations
34. Handmade holiday decorations
35. Handmade sneakers
36. Handmade phone chargers
37. Handmade laptop cases
38. Handmade backpacks
39. Handmade wallets and purses
40. Handmade sports equipment
41. Handmade musical instruments
42. Handmade tools and hardware
43. Handmade outdoor furniture
44. Handmade bedding and linens
45. Handmade carpets and rugs
46. Handmade luggage and travel accessories
47. Handmade pillows and cushions
48. Handmade tech accessories
49. Handmade leather goods
50. Handmade eyewear

Remember to choose a niche that you are passionate about and have knowledge or expertise in.

Chapter 4: Crafting your product

Some tips and techniques for creating high-quality products:

1. Source materials carefully: Choose materials that are high quality and fit your brand's aesthetic. Consider the cost, durability, and sustainability of different materials when making your decision.
2. Pay attention to craftsmanship: Take the time to craft your products with care and attention to detail. This includes using proper tools and techniques, as well as making sure that your products are well-made and visually appealing.
3. Price your products appropriately: Determine the price of your products based on the materials, labor, and overhead costs involved. Make sure to price your products competitively, but also consider the value that your products offer to customers.
4. Take great product photos: High-quality product photos are crucial for attracting customers to your products. Make sure to use good lighting and take photos from multiple angles to showcase your products in the best possible way.

By following these tips, you can create high-quality products that stand out in the market and provide value to your customers. Many websites offer free digital pictures that can be used for various purposes. Here are a few examples:

1. Pexels: Pexels is a website that offers a wide range of high-quality, royalty-free stock photos that can be used for personal or commercial purposes.
2. Unsplash: Unsplash is a website that offers a collection of free, high-resolution photos that can be used for any purpose.

3. Freepik: Freepik is a website that offers a range of free vector graphics, photos, and other design resources that can be used for personal or commercial projects.
4. Pixabay: Pixabay is a website that offers a collection of free photos, vectors, and illustrations that can be used for any purpose, including commercial projects.
5. Canva: Canva is a graphic design platform that offers a range of free images and templates that can be used to create custom designs.

These websites are a great resource for individuals and businesses looking for free digital pictures that can be used for various purposes. It's important to be aware of any licensing or usage restrictions that may apply to the images you use, however, as some images may be subject to copyright or other legal protections.

Canva:

Canva is a graphic design platform that allows users to create a wide range of visual content, including logos, social media graphics, presentations, and more. Many Etsy sellers use Canva to create marketing materials and design elements for their Etsy stores, such as logos, product listings, and promotional graphics. Here are a few reasons why people use Canva with Etsy:

1. Ease of use: Canva is user-friendly and offers a range of templates and design elements that make it easy for people with little to no design experience to create professional-looking graphics.
2. Flexibility: Canva can create a wide range of visual content, making it a versatile tool for Etsy sellers.
3. Cost-effective: Canva offers a free version, as well as paid subscription options, making it a cost-effective option for Etsy sellers who want to create high-quality graphics without breaking the bank.
4. Professional results: Canva's wide range of templates and design elements, as well as its user-friendly interface,

make it possible for users to create professional-looking graphics that can help them stand out on Etsy.

Canva is a popular tool among Etsy sellers due to its ease of use, flexibility, cost-effectiveness, and professional results.
Many companies offer outsourcing services for Etsy sellers. Here is a list of some options:

1. Virtual Assistant Oasis: This company offers various outsourcing services, including customer service, social media management, and product listings.
2. The Etsy VA: This company offers a range of outsourcing services specifically for Etsy sellers, including product research, customer service, and social media management.
3. Etsy Empire: This company offers a range of outsourcing services for Etsy sellers, including product research, customer service, and social media management.
4. The VA Hub: This company offers a range of outsourcing services, including customer service, social media management, and product listings.
5. The Etsy Team: This company offers a range of outsourcing services specifically for Etsy sellers, including customer service, social media management, and product listings.
6. The Etsy Assistant: This company offers a range of outsourcing services specifically for Etsy sellers, including customer service, social media management, and product listings.

Printify:

Printify is an online platform that allows businesses to create and sell custom-printed products such as t-shirts, mugs, and phone cases. The platform integrates with popular online marketplaces such as Etsy, eBay, and Shopify, allowing businesses to easily create and list custom printed products on these platforms.

Printify offers a range of customization options, including the ability to add text, images, and designs to products. The platform also offers a variety of product templates, which can be used to create custom products quickly and easily.

Printify works with a network of manufacturers and fulfillment centers around the world, allowing businesses to choose the location and production method that best suits their needs. The platform handles the production and fulfillment of the products, allowing businesses to focus on marketing and selling their products.

Overall, Printify is a useful tool for businesses that want to create and sell custom printed products on popular online marketplaces such as Etsy, eBay, and Shopify. It offers a range of customization options and handles the production and fulfillment process, making it easy for businesses to create and sell custom products online.

Outsourcing:

Outsourcing is the practice of hiring someone or a company to handle tasks or projects that are typically performed in-house. Here are some tips for outsourcing on Etsy:

1. Define your needs: Before you start outsourcing, it's important to clearly define the tasks or projects that you want to delegate. This will help you find the right service provider and ensure that you get the results you want.
2. Research service providers: Take the time to research and compare different service providers to find the one that best fits your needs and budget. Consider factors such as their expertise, experience, and customer reviews.
3. Communicate clearly: Communicate your expectations and deadlines to the service provider to ensure that they understand your needs and can deliver the results you want.
4. Set up a contract: It's a good idea to set up a contract with the service provider to outline the terms of the agreement, including the scope of work, payment terms, and other relevant details.

5.   Monitor progress: Regularly check in with the service provider to ensure that they are meeting your expectations and meeting their deadlines.

By outsourcing certain tasks to these companies, you can free up time to focus on other aspects of your business, such as creating new products or marketing your store.

Hiring freelancer:

If you are looking to hire freelancers from Fiverr to design products for your Etsy store, here are a few steps you can follow:

1.   Sign up for a Fiverr account: To start using Fiverr, you'll need to create an account. This is a quick and easy process, and you'll need to provide basic information such as your name, email address, and password.
2.   Search for design freelancers: Once you have an account, you can start searching for design freelancers on Fiverr. You can use the search bar to enter keywords related to the design services you need, and you'll be presented with a list of freelancers who offer those services. You can also use the advanced search options to narrow down your search results based on location, language, and price.
3.   Review profiles and portfolios: Once you have a list of potential freelancers, you can review their profiles and portfolios to get a sense of their skills and experience. Pay attention to the reviews and ratings from other clients, as well as the samples of work that the freelancer has included in their portfolio.
4.   Contact the freelancer: Once you've identified a freelancer who seems like a good fit for your needs, you can contact them through the Fiverr platform to discuss your project in more detail. You can use the messaging system to communicate with the freelancer and ask any questions you may have.
5.   Place an order: If you decide to hire a freelancer, you can place an order through the Fiverr platform. You'll need to

provide details about your project, including the scope of work, deadlines, and any specific requirements you may have.

Overall, hiring freelancers from Fiverr is a straightforward process that allows you to easily connect with professionals who can help you design products for your Etsy store.

There are several free online graphic editors that you can use to create and edit images for your Etsy store. Here are a few options:

1. Canva: This graphic design platform offers a range of templates and tools for creating and editing images, including logos, social media graphics, and product listings.
2. Adobe Spark: This graphic design platform offers a range of templates and tools for creating and editing images, including logos, social media graphics, and product listings.
3. Piktochart: This graphic design platform offers a range of templates and tools for creating and editing images, including infographics, presentations, and social media graphics.
4. GIMP: This open-source image editing software offers a range of tools for editing and retouching images, including resizing, cropping, and color correction.

By using these online graphic editors, you can easily create and edit images for your Etsy store without the need for expensive software. These platforms can be accessed from any computer with an internet connection, making them a convenient option for creating and editing images on the go.

Drop shipping is a business model where a seller partners with a supplier who manufactures and ships the products directly to the customer. Here is a list of some drop shipping companies that work with Etsy sellers:

1. Oberlo: This platform allows Etsy sellers to connect with suppliers and import products directly into their Etsy store.
2. Doba: This platform allows Etsy sellers to browse a catalog of products from multiple suppliers and choose which products to list in their store.
3. Wholesale2B: This platform allows Etsy sellers to access a catalog of products from multiple suppliers and automate listing and fulfilling orders.
4. SaleHoo: This platform allows Etsy sellers to access a directory of suppliers and connect with them to source products for their stores.
5. Sunrise Wholesale: This company offers a range of products, including home decor, outdoor gear, and electronics, that Etsy sellers can list in their store and have shipped directly to their customers.

Using these drop shipping companies, Etsy sellers can offer a wider range of products without having to hold inventory or manage the fulfillment process themselves. However, it's important to carefully research and vet any drop shipping company before partnering with them to ensure they are reliable and trustworthy.
Digital art downloads on Etsy are digital files that customers can purchase and download from an Etsy seller's store. These files may include artwork, graphics, patterns, or other digital design elements that customers can use for personal or commercial purposes.
Examples of digital art downloads on Etsy include:

1. Digital art prints: These are digital versions of art prints that customers can purchase and download to print themselves or use as digital wallpapers or backgrounds.
2. Digital clip art: These are digital graphics that customers can purchase and download to use in their own projects, such as invitations, logos, or other design elements.
3. Digital paper packs: These are digital collections of patterns or textures that customers can purchase and download to use in their own projects, such as invitations, scrapbooking, or other crafts.

4. Digital coloring pages: These are digital versions of coloring pages that customers can purchase and download to print and color themselves.

By offering digital art downloads on Etsy, sellers can reach a global audience and generate passive income as customers continue to purchase and download their products over time.

Trademarks Rules and Regulation

Trademarks are distinctive signs, symbols, or words that identify and distinguish a particular product or service from others. In the United States, the protection of trademarks is governed by federal and state laws, as well as international treaties.
To qualify for trademark protection in the United States, a trademark must be used in connection with the sale of goods or services, and it must be distinctive. This means that the trademark must be capable of distinguishing the goods or services of one company from those of another.
Trademarks can be registered with the United States Patent and Trademark Office (USPTO), which is the federal agency responsible for granting trademarks. The USPTO will review the trademark application to ensure that it meets all of the necessary legal requirements and that it is not already being used by another company. If the trademark is approved, it will be registered, and the owner will receive a certificate of registration.
Trademarks are important because they allow companies to protect their brand identity and reputation, and they can be valuable assets for businesses. It's important for companies to carefully consider their trademarks and to take steps to protect them through registration and proper use.

Chapter 5: Marketing your shop

There are several ways to market your products on Etsy:

1. Optimize your listings: Make sure that your listings are optimized for search engines by using relevant keywords in your titles, descriptions, and tags. This will make it easier for potential customers to find your products when searching on Etsy.
2. Use social media: Share your products and promotions on social media platforms like Instagram, Facebook, TikTok, and Pinterest to attract more customers. You can also join relevant social media groups and communities related to your niche to connect with potential customers.
3. Offer discounts and promotions: Consider offering discounts or promotions to encourage sales. You could offer a discount code to your email subscribers or run a sale in your shop.
4. Collaborate with other sellers: Collaborating with other Etsy sellers can be a great way to reach new customers. You could consider collaborating on a joint product or hosting a giveaway together.
5. Participate in Etsy events: Etsy hosts various events, including Etsy Made Local, which allows you to sell your products in person at local events. Participating in these events can be a great way to meet potential customers and showcase your products.
6. Offer excellent customer service: Providing excellent customer service is crucial for building customer loyalty and attracting positive reviews. Respond promptly to customer inquiries, and go above and beyond to ensure that your customers are happy with their purchases.
7. Use paid advertising: Etsy offers paid advertising options, including promoted listings and Google AdWords, which can help increase the visibility of your products.

As your shop grows, it's important to stay organized and efficient to keep up with orders and customer inquiries. Here are a few tips to help you do this:

1. Use a calendar to keep track of deadlines and important dates.

2. Set up automated emails for common customer inquiries, like shipping information and returns.
3. Use a system for managing orders, such as a spreadsheet or a task management app.
4. Outsource tasks you don't have time for, like shipping and product photography.

By implementing these marketing strategies, you can increase the visibility of your products and attract more customers to your Etsy shop.
Search engine optimization (SEO) improves the visibility of a website or online store in search engines like Google. Here are some tips for maximizing your marketing efforts with SEO:

1. Research keywords: Use keyword research tools to find keywords that are relevant to your products and business. Include these keywords in your website and product titles, descriptions, and tags to help search engines understand the content of your site.
2. Use high-quality content: Create high-quality, informative content that includes relevant keywords. This can help improve your search engine rankings and attract more visitors to your site.
3. Use alt tags: Use alt tags to describe the images on your website and include relevant keywords. This can help search engines understand the content of your images and improve your search rankings.
4. Use social media: Use social media platforms, such as Instagram, Twitter, and Facebook, to promote your products and website. This can help drive traffic to your site and improve your search rankings.
5. Use backlinks: Obtain backlinks from high-quality, relevant websites to your site. This can help improve your search rankings and increase the authority of your website.

By following these tips, you can effectively use SEO to improve the visibility of your website or online store and maximize your marketing efforts.

Keywords are terms that people use when searching for products online. Using the right keywords in your product listings can help improve your visibility and attract the right customers to your products. Here are a few tips for choosing the best keywords for t-shirt products:

1. Use specific terms: Instead of using general terms like "t-shirt," consider using more specific keywords that describe your t-shirts, such as "women's graphic t-shirt" or "men's vintage t-shirt."
2. Include product features: Consider the features of your t-shirts that may be important to customers, such as the material, fit, or design, and include these as keywords in your listings.
3. Consider seasonality: If your t-shirts are suitable for specific seasons or events, include keywords that reflect this, such as "summer t-shirt" or "Valentine's Day t-shirt."
4. Use popular search terms: Use tools like the Etsy search bar and Google's keyword planner to research popular search terms and see which ones are relevant to your products.

By using specific, descriptive keywords that reflect the features and relevance of your t-shirts, you can help attract the right customers to your products on Etsy.

Here are more examples of keywords that you could use when selling t-shirts on Etsy:

1. "Women's t-shirt"
2. "Men's t-shirt"
3. "Graphic t-shirt"
4. "Vintage t-shirt"
5. "Custom t-shirt"
6. "Personalized t-shirt"
7. "Funny t-shirt"
8. "Trendy t-shirt"
9. "Comfortable t-shirt"
10. "Soft t-shirt"

11. "Cotton t-shirt"
12. "Bamboo t-shirt"
13. "Sustainable t-shirt"
14. "Eco-friendly t-shirt"
15. "Organic t-shirt"

In addition to these general keywords, it's also a good idea to include specific details about your t-shirts, such as the material, fit, design, and unique features.

Here are a few examples of keywords that you could use when selling mugs on Etsy:

1. "Coffee mug"
2. "Tea mug"
3. "Ceramic mug"
4. "Travel mug"
5. "Custom mug"
6. "Personalized mug"
7. "Funny mug"
8. "Unique mug"
9. "Gift mug"
10. "Wedding mug"
11. "Birthday mug"
12. "Mother's Day mug"
13. "Father's Day mug"
14. "Valentine's Day mug"
15. "Christmas mug"

In addition to these general keywords, it's also a good idea to include specific details about your mugs, such as the material, size, design, and unique features. This will help you attract the right customers to your products on Etsy.

Here are a few examples of keywords that you could use when selling wall art on Etsy:

1. "Wall art"
2. "Canvas art"

3. "Printed art"
4. "Abstract art"
5. "Landscape art"
6. "Flower art"
7. "Animal art"
8. "Nature art"
9. "Custom art"
10. "Personalized art"
11. "Funny art"
12. "Unique art"
13. "Gift art"
14. "Wedding art"
15. "Home decor art"

Advertise your Etsy store on TikTok:

1. Create short, engaging videos: TikTok is all about short, catchy videos, so make sure to create content that is attention-grabbing and visually appealing. You could show off your products, share behind-the-scenes footage of your business, or create tutorials related to your niche.
2. Use relevant hashtags: Use relevant hashtags to make it easier for people to discover your content. You can use hashtags related to your products or niche, as well as popular TikTok hashtags like #etsyseller or #handmade.
3. Collaborate with influencers: Consider collaborating with TikTok influencers who have a large following in your niche. You could send them a product to review or create a challenge together to promote your store.
4. Use paid advertising: TikTok offers paid advertising options, including promoted hashtags and in-feed ads, which can help increase the visibility of your content.
5. Engage with your followers: Make sure to engage with your followers and respond to comments and messages. Building a community of loyal followers can help drive sales and promote your store on TikTok.

By following these tips, you can effectively advertise your Etsy store on TikTok and reach a new audience of potential customers.

Advertise your Etsy store on Facebook:

1. Set up a Facebook business page: First, create a Facebook business page for your Etsy store. This will allow you to showcase your products, share updates and promotions, and interact with your customers.
2. Use Facebook ads: Facebook offers a variety of paid advertising options, including sponsored posts and targeted ads. You can use these to increase the visibility of your products and reach a specific audience.
3. Share updates and promotions: Share updates and promotions on your Facebook page to keep your followers informed and encourage sales. You could offer discounts, run contests, or showcase new products.
4. Engage with your followers: Make sure to respond to comments and messages from your followers and engage with them regularly. Building a community of loyal followers can help drive sales and promote your store on Facebook.
5. Use relevant hashtags: Use relevant hashtags in your posts to make it easier for people to discover your content. You can use hashtags related to your products or niche, as well as popular Facebook hashtags like #etsyseller or #handmade.

By following these tips, you can effectively advertise your Etsy store on Facebook and reach a new audience of potential customers.

1. Set up a Google Ads account: To use Google Ads, you will need to create a Google Ads account. You can do this by going to the Google Ads website and clicking on the "Start now" button.
2. Choose your campaign type: Google Ads offers a variety of campaign types to choose from, including search ads, display ads, and shopping ads. Select the campaign type that best fits your business goals and target audience.
3. Set up your campaign: Follow the prompts to set up your campaign, including choosing your target audience, budget, and ad placements. You will also need to create your ad copy and select the keywords or topics you want to target.
4. Link your Etsy store: To link your Etsy store to your Google Ads account, you will need to connect your Google Ads, and Etsy accounts through the Google Ads integration in your Etsy shop settings.
5. Monitor and optimize your campaign: Once your campaign is live, be sure to monitor its performance and make any necessary adjustments to optimize its effectiveness. You can do this by analyzing your ad's performance data, such as clicks and conversions, and making changes to your targeting, budget, or ad copy as needed.

By following these steps, you can effectively advertise your Etsy store with Google Ads and reach a new audience of potential customers.

Chapter 6: Growing your business

Several websites offer shipping services for Etsy sellers. Here are a few examples:

1. USPS: The United States Postal Service (USPS) is a government agency that provides a range of shipping services for individuals and businesses. Etsy sellers can use USPS to ship their products to customers within the United States and internationally.
2. UPS: UPS is a global shipping and logistics company that offers a range of shipping services for businesses. Etsy sellers can use UPS to ship their products to customers within the United States and internationally.
3. FedEx: FedEx is a global shipping and logistics company that offers a range of shipping services for businesses. Etsy sellers can use FedEx to ship their products to customers within the United States and internationally.
4. DHL: DHL is a global shipping and logistics company that offers a range of shipping services for businesses. Etsy sellers can use DHL to ship their products to customers within the United States and internationally.

These shipping companies offer a range of options for Etsy sellers looking to ship their products to customers. It's important to carefully consider factors such as cost, delivery times, and the size and weight of the products when choosing a shipping service.

Once you have a successful Etsy shop, you may consider expanding your business. This could involve adding new products, opening a physical storefront, or partnering with other businesses.

To add new products, consider what your customers are asking for or what gaps exist in your current product line. You can also research trends in your industry to find new ideas.

Here are some tips for growing your business on Etsy:

1. Offer high-quality products: Make sure to offer high-quality products that are well-made and meet the needs of your customers. Consider sourcing materials and supplies carefully to ensure that your products are of the highest quality.
2. Use good product photography: Use high-quality photos to showcase your products in the best light. Use good lighting and a plain background, and consider using multiple angles to show off the different features of your products.

3. Write compelling product descriptions: Use descriptive language and highlight the unique features and benefits of your products in your product descriptions. Consider using keywords to help your products appear in search results.
4. Offer excellent customer service: Respond to customer inquiries and reviews in a timely and professional manner, and make sure to resolve any issues promptly. Building a positive reputation with your customers can help drive sales and increase customer loyalty.
5. Utilize social media: Use social media platforms, such as Instagram, Twitter, and Facebook, to promote your products and connect with potential customers. You can also use hashtags and participate in relevant conversations to increase your visibility.
6. Consider offering customizations: Allow customers to customize your products by offering different colors, sizes, or personalized engravings. This can help increase sales and customer satisfaction.
7. Expand your product line: Consider adding new products to your store to keep your offerings fresh and attract new customers.

By following these tips, you can grow your business on Etsy and reach a wider audience of potential customers.

Etsy is an online marketplace that allows you to sell your products to a global audience without needing a separate website. If you choose to sell on Etsy, you do not need to worry about hosting your own website.

However, if you want to create a separate website in addition to your Etsy store, you will need to find a website hosting provider. There are many websites hosting providers to choose from, and the right one for you will depend on your specific needs and budget.

Some popular website hosting providers include:

1. Bluehost: This hosting provider offers a range of plans for small and medium-sized businesses, including shared hosting, VPS hosting, and dedicated hosting.
2. HostGator: This hosting provider offers a range of plans for small and medium-sized businesses, including shared hosting, VPS hosting, and dedicated hosting.
3. SiteGround: This hosting provider offers a range of plans for small and medium-sized businesses, including shared hosting, cloud hosting, and dedicated hosting.
4. A2 Hosting: This hosting provider offers a range of plans for small and medium-sized businesses, including shared hosting, VPS hosting, and dedicated hosting.

By choosing a reputable hosting provider, you can ensure that your website is reliable and performs well for your customers.
There are several ways that you can generate passive income on Etsy:

1. Create digital products: Offer digital products, such as printables or digital art, that can be easily downloaded by customers. This can generate passive income as customers continue to purchase your products over time.
2. Sell physical products through dropshipping: Partner with a dropshipping supplier to offer physical products on your Etsy store. This can allow you to generate passive income without the need to hold inventory or manage the fulfillment process.
3. Offer subscriptions: Consider offering a subscription service for your products, such as a monthly box of handmade items. This can generate passive income as customers continue to pay for the subscription over time.
4. Create an affiliate program: Partner with other businesses or influencers to promote your products on your Etsy

store. You can offer a commission for each sale made through the affiliate program, generating passive income as customers make purchases through your store.

Etsy's affiliate program allows individuals and organizations to earn a commission by promoting Etsy products on their websites, social media accounts, or other online platforms.
To participate in the Etsy affiliate program, you'll need to sign up for an account and be accepted. Once accepted, you'll be given access to a range of resources, including links and banners that you can use to promote Etsy products. When a customer clicks on one of your links and makes a purchase on Etsy, you'll earn a commission on the sale.
The Etsy affiliate program is a good way for individuals and organizations with an online presence to earn extra income by promoting handmade, vintage, and creative goods on Etsy. It's also a great way for Etsy sellers to promote their own products and potentially increase their sales.
Many companies work with Etsy, including:

1. Printful: This company offers on-demand printing and fulfillment services for Etsy sellers.
2. Doba: This company offers a drop shipping platform for Etsy sellers.
3. Wholesale2B: This company offers a drop shipping platform for Etsy sellers.
4. Worldwide Brands: This company offers a directory of wholesalers and drop shippers for Etsy sellers.
5. Modalyst: This company offers a drop shipping platform for Etsy sellers.
6. Spocket: This company offers a drop shipping platform for Etsy sellers.
7. Megagoods: This company offers a drop shipping platform for Etsy sellers.
8. Sunrise Wholesale: This company offers a drop shipping platform for Etsy sellers.
9. SaleHoo: This company offers a directory of wholesalers and drop shippers for Etsy sellers.

By working with these companies, Etsy sellers can access a wide range of products and fulfillment services to help grow their businesses. It's important to carefully research and compares the different options to find the best fit for your business needs and goals.

Canva is a graphic design platform that allows users to create a wide range of visual content, including:

1. Logos
2. Social media graphics
3. Business cards
4. Posters
5. Presentations
6. Brochures
7. Flyers
8. Invitations
9. Infographics
10. Email headers
11. Website graphics
12. YouTube banners
13. Podcast covers
14. Ebook covers

In addition to these types of content, Canva also offers a range of templates and design elements that can be used to create custom graphics for various purposes. Some common use cases for Canva include creating marketing materials for businesses, designing event materials, and creating personal projects such as scrapbooks and photo collages. Overall, Canva is a versatile tool that can create a wide range of visual content for personal and professional use.

Chapter 7: Words of Wisdom

Etsy pays sellers on a weekly basis, with payments being released on Monday mornings (Eastern Time).

To receive payment, sellers must have a valid payment method with Etsy. Payment methods available to sellers include direct deposit, PayPal, and check. Sellers can choose their preferred payment method and update it anytime through their account settings.

It's important to note that Etsy may hold payment for a period of time after a sale has been made. This is to allow time for the buyer to return the item or file a claim if there is an issue with the order. Once the hold period has passed, the payment will be released to the seller.

Etsy's weekly payment schedule allows sellers to receive their earnings in a timely manner and helps them to manage their finances effectively.

It is difficult to provide a specific graph of the profitability of selling on Etsy, as profitability can vary widely depending on a number of factors, such as the type of products being sold, the seller's pricing and marketing strategies, and the overall demand for the products.

That being said, there are a few general trends that can be observed when it comes to selling on Etsy. For example, it is generally easier to be profitable on Etsy if you focus on selling unique, high-quality products in demand. It is also important to have a strong marketing strategy in place to reach potential customers and be competitive with your pricing.

The profitability of selling on Etsy will depend on a number of factors, and it may take some trial and error to find the right mix of products, pricing, and marketing strategies that work for your business.

Yes, it is possible for an inexperienced person to become a successful seller on Etsy. However, it will likely require much hard work, dedication, and learning to build and grow a successful business. Here are a few things that can help an inexperienced person become a successful seller on Etsy:

1. Research and education: Take the time to research and learn about the online marketplace and the niche you are interested in. Find resources such as online courses, podcasts, and blogs to help you build your knowledge and skills.
2. Network and seek advice: Reach out to other Etsy sellers, especially those who are successful in your niche, and ask for advice and guidance. Join Etsy seller groups and forums to connect with other sellers and learn from their experiences.

3. Be consistent and persistent: Building a successful business on Etsy takes time and effort. Be consistent in your efforts, and don't give up easily. Keep learning and adapting to improve your products and marketing efforts.
4. Offer high-quality products and customer service: It's important to focus on offering high-quality products and excellent customer service to build a positive reputation and attract repeat customers.

By following these tips and being willing to work, an inexperienced person can become a successful seller on Etsy.

Chapter 8: Tips and Tricks to maximize profit

Example of an inviting product listing description for a handmade jewelry item:

Welcome to my shop! This beautiful necklace is made with genuine turquoise beads and handmade silver wire. The necklace is 18 inches long and has a lobster clasp closure. The turquoise beads have a stunning blue color that complements any outfit. This necklace is perfect for everyday wear or for dressing up an evening look. Each necklace is made with care and attention to detail, so you can be sure you are getting a high-quality piece. Thank you for considering this handmade jewelry item. I hope you love it as much as I do!
In this example, the seller uses descriptive language to highlight the unique features of the necklace and create a sense of value for the customer. They also use a friendly and welcoming tone to encourage the customer to purchase the item. By writing an inviting product listing description, you can increase the chances of making a sale and creating a positive impression on potential customers.

Example of a product listing description for a t-shirt with a print design:

Add some style to your wardrobe with this trendy t-shirt! The shirt is made of soft, high-quality cotton and features a unique graphic print design sure to turn heads. The shirt has a relaxed fit and a classic crew neck, making it comfortable to wear all day long. Whether you're running errands or hanging out with friends, this shirt is sure to become a staple in your wardrobe. The shirt is available in various sizes, so you can find the perfect fit. Don't wait – order yours today and make a statement with this stylish t-shirt! In this example, the seller uses descriptive language to highlight the features and benefits of the t-shirt, such as the high-quality materials and unique design. They also encourage the customer to take action by urging them to order the shirt before it's gone. By writing a compelling product listing description, you can increase the chances of making a sale that attracts potential customers to your store.

Example of a product listing description for a handmade item:

Introducing our newest addition to the shop – this beautiful handmade ceramic vase. Each vase is made by hand using high-quality clay and glazed with a glossy finish. The vase has a unique shape and texture, making it a one-of-a-kind piece that is sure to add character to any room. The vase is perfect for displaying flowers or simply as a decorative piece. Each vase is handmade with care and attention to detail, so you can be sure you are getting a high-quality piece. Thank you for considering this handmade vase. I hope you love it as much as I do!
In this example, the seller uses descriptive language to highlight the unique features and handmade nature of the vase and also conveys a sense of pride and care in creating the item. By highlighting the handmade aspect of the product, the seller is able to create a sense of value and appeal to customers who are looking for unique, handmade items.

Add some color to your walls with this beautiful art print! The print features a vibrant abstract design that will make a statement in any space. The print is produced using high-quality archival inks and paper, ensuring that the colors remain vibrant and the print remains of the highest quality. The print is available in various sizes to fit any space and is shipped rolled in a protective tube to ensure it arrives in perfect condition. Thank you for considering this art print. I hope it brings joy and inspiration to your home or office!

In this example, the seller uses descriptive language to highlight the features and benefits of the art print, such as the high-quality materials and vibrant design. They also provide information about the shipping process to reassure the customer that the print will arrive in good condition. By writing a compelling product listing description, you can increase the chances of making a sale and attracting potential customers to your store.

Here are 14 ideas for generating additional income on Etsy:

1. Offer customizations: Allow customers to customize your products by offering different colors, sizes, or personalized engravings.
2. Sell digital products: In addition to physical products, consider offering digital products, such as printable art, digital planners, or ebooks.
3. Sell wholesale: Sell your products in bulk to other businesses or individuals who resell them.
4. Offer subscriptions: Consider offering a subscription service, where customers can receive regular deliveries of your products.
5. Offer bundle deals: Create bundle deals by grouping together several of your products and offering them at a discounted price.

6. Sell used or vintage items: In addition to handmade or new items, consider selling used or vintage items in good condition.

7. Sell supplies: In addition to finished products, consider selling the supplies and materials you use to create your products.

8. Sell patterns: If you create handmade items, consider selling patterns or tutorials for others to make similar items.

9. Sell services: Offer services related to your products, such as repair or customization services.

10. Sell gift cards: Offer gift cards for your shop, which can be used to purchase any of your products.

11. Sell on other platforms: Consider selling your products on other platforms, such as Amazon or your own website.

12. Sell secondhand items: In addition to handmade or new items, consider selling secondhand items in good condition.

13. Sell bulk quantities: In addition to individual items, consider selling your products in bulk quantities.

14. Sell gift sets: Create gift sets by grouping together several of your products and packaging them in an attractive way.

Some tips for selling digital art on Etsy:

1. Choose a niche: Choose a niche or category for your digital art that you are passionate about and have knowledge or expertise in. This will help you create unique and high-quality art that stands out in the market.

2. Create a brand: Develop a brand identity for your digital art, including a logo, color scheme, and style. This will help you create a cohesive look for your art and establish a professional image.

3. Research your competition: Research other digital art sellers on Etsy to see what types of art and prices they are

offering. This will help you understand the market and create a competitive pricing strategy.

4. Create high-quality art: Make sure to create high-quality art that is visually appealing and reflects your brand's style. Consider using professional software and equipment to create your art.

5. Set up your store: Set up your store on Etsy by creating a seller account and listing your digital art. Be sure to include detailed descriptions, high-quality preview images, and accurate pricing for your art.

6. Promote your store: Promote your store through social media, email marketing, and other channels to reach a wider audience. Consider offering discounts or promotions to encourage sales.

7. Engage with your customers: Make sure to respond to customer inquiries and reviews in a timely and professional manner. Building a positive reputation with your customers can help drive sales and increase customer loyalty.

An example of an outsourcing contract:

[Company Name] (the "Company") is hiring [Service Provider Name] (the "Service Provider") to perform the following services:
[Insert a detailed description of the services to be provided, including any specific tasks, deadlines, and deliverables.]
The Company will pay the Service Provider the following fee for the services:
[Insert the fee amount and any relevant payment terms, such as a flat fee, hourly rate, or milestone payments.]
The term of this contract is [insert the start and end dates of the contract].
The Company and the Service Provider agree to the following terms and conditions:
[Insert any additional terms and conditions, such as confidentiality, intellectual property ownership, indemnification, and termination provisions.]
This contract constitutes the entire agreement between the Company and the Service Provider, and supersedes any prior

agreements or understandings, whether written or oral. This
contract may not be amended or modified except in writing, signed
by both parties.
This contract shall be governed by the laws of the [insert state or
country]. Any disputes arising under or in connection with this
contract shall be resolved by [insert method of dispute resolution,
such as arbitration or litigation].
IN WITNESS WHEREOF, the parties have executed this contract
as of the date first above written.
[Insert company name]
[Insert service provider name]
[Insert company signature]
[Insert service provider signature]
This is just an example of an outsourcing contract and should not
be used as a template without consulting with a lawyer. It's
essential to carefully customize the contract to fit the specific needs
and goals of your business.

Ten tips for taking the best pictures to list on Etsy:

1. Use good lighting: Make sure to use natural or artificial lighting that is bright and evenly distributed. Avoid using flash, as it can create harsh shadows and distort colors.
2. Use a tripod: A tripod can help you take steady, blur-free photos, especially if you use a DSLR camera.
3. Use a plain background: Choose a plain, uncluttered background to make your product the focus of the photo. A solid color or textured background works well.
4. Use multiple angles: Take photos from multiple angles to show off the different features of your product. This can include close-ups, full-length shots, and shots from above or below.
5. Edit your photos: Use photo editing software to adjust the lighting, color, and sharpness of your photos to make them look their best.
6. Use a high resolution: Make sure to use a high resolution when taking your photos to ensure that they look sharp and clear when displayed on Etsy.

7. Use a consistent style: Use a consistent style and lighting setup for all of your product photos to create a cohesive look.

8. Use props: Consider using props, such as flowers or other objects, to add interest to your photos and give context to your products.

9. Take close-ups: Take close-up shots to show off the details and textures of your products.

10. Use a model: If appropriate, consider using a model to show off your products in use or to give scale to your products.

By following these tips, you can take high-quality photos that showcase your products in the best light and attract potential customers to your Etsy shop.